You and th
U.S. Governm

Jennifer Overend Prior, Ph.D.

Consultants

Shelley Scudder
Gifted Education Teacher
Broward County Schools

Caryn Williams, M.S.Ed.
Madison County Schools
Huntsville, AL

Publishing Credits

Conni Medina, M.A.Ed., *Managing Editor*
Lee Aucoin, *Creative Director*
Torrey Maloof, *Editor*
Marissa Rodriguez, *Designer*
Stephanie Reid, *Photo Editor*
Rachelle Cracchiolo, M.S.Ed., *Publisher*

Image Credits: Cover, pp. 1, 4–5, 5, 9, 12, 17 Getty Images; pp. 7, 18, 24–25, 25 Alamy; p. 19 Associated Press; p. 29 (top) Frances M. Roberts/Newscom; pp. 22, 26, 27, 28 iStockphoto; p. 15 REUTERS/Newscom; pp. 6–7, 14–15 The Granger Collection; p. 10 The Library of Congress [LC-USZC2-2444]; pp. 8, 32 Tim Bradley; All other images from Shutterstock.

Teacher Created Materials
5301 Oceanus Drive
Huntington Beach, CA 92649-1030
http://www.tcmpub.com

ISBN 978-1-4333-6993-3

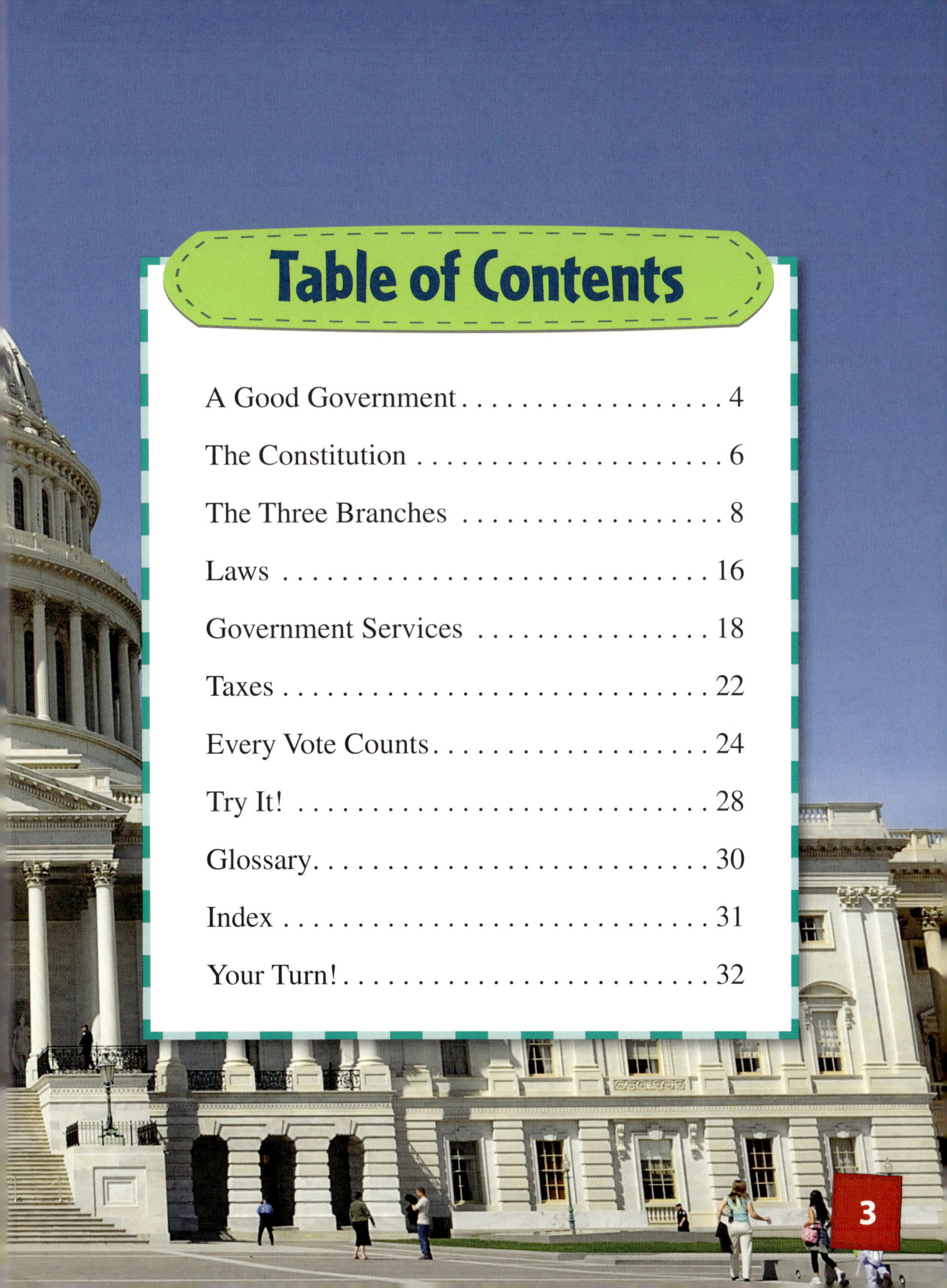

Table of Contents

Government leaders meet to talk about our country.

A Good Government

One person can do great things. But when people work together, they can do even bigger things. A good **government** (GUHV-ern-muhnt) helps people work and live together. It keeps people safe. And it makes the laws that help a country run smoothly.

American citizens vote for their leaders.

There are different types of government. The United States government is a **democracy** (dih-MOK-ruh-see). This means that United States **citizens** (SIT-uh-zuhns) vote for, or choose, their leaders. Citizens are people who belong to a country.

The Constitution

America declared its independence (in-di-PEN-duhns), or freedom, in 1776. It had to fight in a war called the *American Revolution* (rev-uh-LOO-shuhn). This was a war with Great Britain for America's freedom. In 1783, the United States won the war. A new country was born.

America's leaders write the Constitution in 1787.

The new country needed laws. It also needed a fair government. In 1787, America's leaders wrote the Constitution (kon-sti-TOO-shuhn). This **document** (DOK-yuh-muhnt) says how the government should work. It is the main set of laws for our country. It tells how people should choose leaders. It explains how much power the government can have and how it should run.

This is the Constitution.

America's Leaders

Early America had many important leaders. People such as John Adams, Samuel Adams, Benjamin Franklin, Thomas Jefferson, and George Washington all helped make America what it is today.

The Three Branches

Our government is made up of three parts called *branches*. They are like legs on a stool. Each leg is different. But they are all part of the same stool. If one leg is taken away, the stool will not stand.

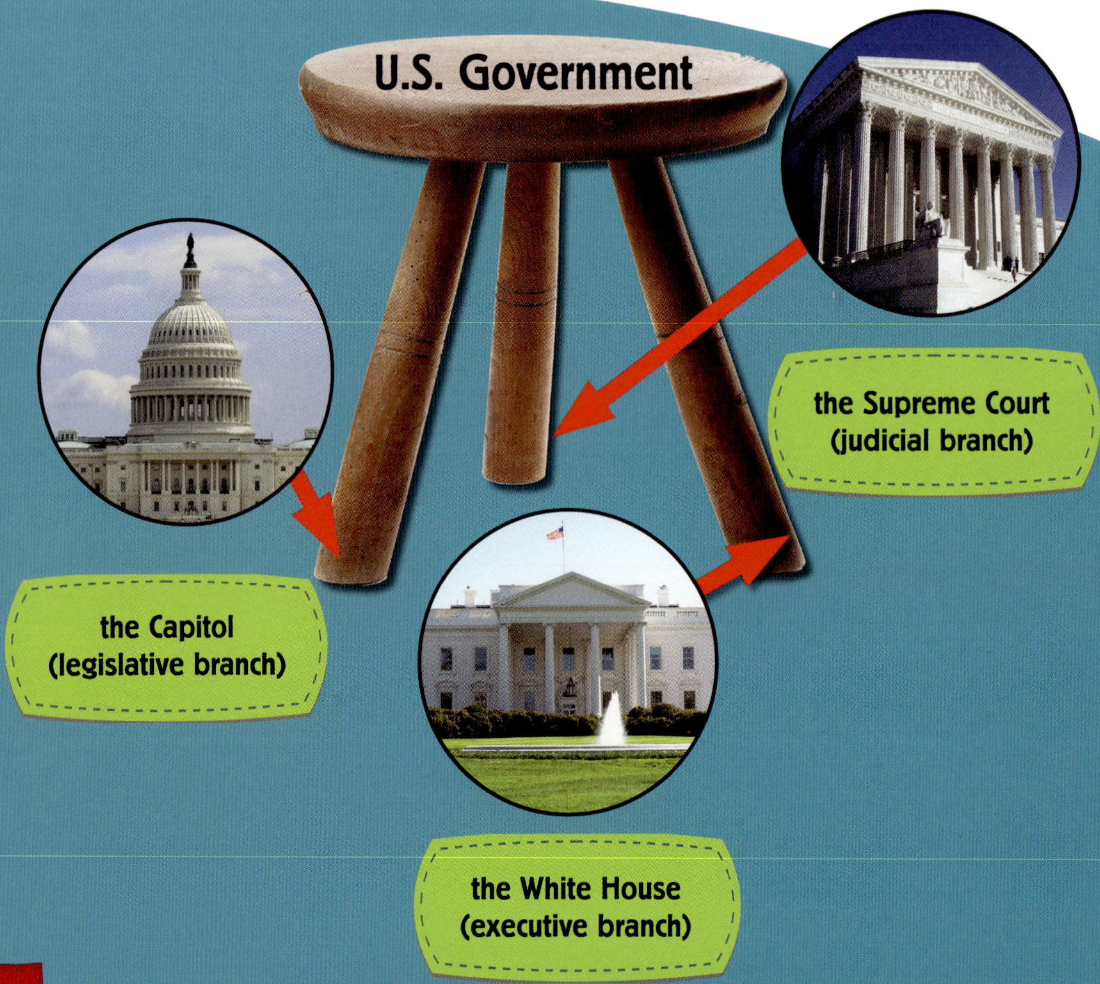

In the U.S. government, each branch balances the others. And each branch makes sure the other branches do their jobs well. Every branch has an important role to play. But no branch has too much power. The three branches are the executive (ig-ZEK-you-tiv) branch, the legislative (LEJ-is-ley-tiv) branch, and the judicial (joo-DISH-uhl) branch.

From City to Country

The president leads the country. A governor leads a state. A mayor leads a city. These people help our country run smoothly.

The mayor of New York City reads a book to kids in 2007.

The Executive Branch

Every group needs a leader. Things work better when someone is in charge. A principal leads a school. A coach leads a team. The president is the leader of our country. The executive branch is made up of the president and vice president.

George Washington was the first president of the United States.

The executive branch makes sure laws are followed. The president approves new laws. He or she makes big decisions for the country. The vice president becomes president if the president can no longer do the job.

Every Four Years

Americans vote for a president every four years.

This is the White House. The president lives and works here.

The Legislative Branch

Citizens need people to represent them in the government. So they vote for **representatives** (rep-ri-ZEN-tuh-tivs). They make sure the government meets the citizens' needs. The representatives make up the legislative branch.

This is a meeting of Congress.

There are two parts to the legislative branch. There is the Senate and the House of Representatives. Together, they are called Congress (KONG-gris). Congress writes laws. A new idea for a law is called a *bill*. A certain number of representatives need to vote for a bill. Then, the bill is sent to the president to approve.

President Roosevelt signs a bill in 1936.

The Judicial Branch

Congress is careful when writing new laws. But sometimes, it is hard to know when a law is unfair or when it has been broken. The judicial branch makes sure the laws are fair.

The Supreme Court

The Supreme Court is the highest court in the United States. This means that all the other courts in the country need to follow its decisions. The judges in the Supreme Court are called *justices*.

This is the inside of the Supreme Court.

The judicial branch is made up of **judges** (JUHJ-iz). It is their job to listen to arguments about laws. They decide when laws are being broken. They also make sure laws follow the Constitution.

These are the justices of the Supreme Court in 2013.

Laws help keep us safe on the road.

Laws

Imagine there were no laws. If there were no laws, then there would be no order. People might make poor choices. Laws say how fast cars can drive and how old a person needs to be to vote. Laws help protect people and keep them safe. It is important for people to follow the laws.

The police officer writes a ticket for someone who has broken the law.

The government makes sure laws are followed. It decides what the **consequences** (KON-si-kwen-siz) are if people do not follow the laws. People may have to pay fines. This means they give money to the government. Or they may have to spend time in jail.

Government Services

The government provides many services. These services are open to the public. This means that everyone can use them. The government pays for many schools, libraries, and parks.

These kids watch a puppet show at their public library.

Students can learn at public schools for free. People can read books from a public library for no charge. Kids can play at a public park without having to pay money. These services are for everyone in a community to use.

These workers are building a public park.

These firefighters are putting out a fire in a building.

Emergency (ih-MUR-juhn-see) services are also paid for by the government. These include police officers and firefighters. If you are in danger, you can ask them for help. They keep people safe.

These people are using public transportation.

Public **transportation** (trans-per-TEY-shuhn) is a government service, too. Public transportation includes things such as buses and trains. The government also pays for the roads and rails on which the buses and trains ride.

Taxes

All these government services cost money. In most states, people pay taxes on things they buy. For example, if you buy a book, you may pay a few extra cents in taxes. That extra cost is a tax. The money goes to the government to pay for services.

We pay taxes on things we buy, such as books.

Every adult who makes money pays taxes. Taxes make things cost more money. But taxes pay for many things we use every day.

Taxes pay to fix roads.

Every Vote Counts

In the United States, we choose our government leaders by voting. The people who get the most votes win. They get to be the leaders. They represent the citizens of our country. Citizens who are over 18 years old can vote.

These citizens are voting.

It is important that every citizen votes. Voting lets us choose the people who will make decisions for our country. If people do not like the choices a leader makes, they can vote for a new leader.

Elections

Government leaders are chosen in elections (ih-LEK-shuhns). In an election, citizens vote by using a ballot. Some ballots are paper. Others are electronic (ih-lek-TRON-ik). Ballots are kept secret. This is so people can vote honestly. They do not have to worry about what others will think.

This is a ballot.

You may be too young to vote. But that does not mean you are too young to make a difference. Talk with your family. Find out what they think about the government. Make sure the adults you know are ready to vote. Tell them why it is important to vote.

This girl is helping others by giving things to people who need them.

There are many ways to be a good citizen. Learn about the services that are important to you. Follow the laws of our country. Help others in need. Good citizens can make a great country.

These people help keep their community clean by picking up trash.

Try It!

Get involved! Make a list of three things you can do to be a good citizen. Share your list with a parent. Have an adult help you do one thing on your list.

These girls help an elderly citizen shop.

These kids plant a new garden in their city.

This boy recycles.

Glossary

citizens—members of a country or place

consequences—the results or effects of someone's actions and choices

democracy—a form of government in which people choose leaders by voting

document—an official paper that gives information about something

emergency—an unexpected and usually dangerous situation that calls for urgent help

government—a group of leaders who make choices for a country

judges—people who have the power to make decisions on cases brought before a court of law

representatives—people who act or speak for another person or group

transportation—cars, trucks, buses, and other moving vehicles

Index

Your Turn!

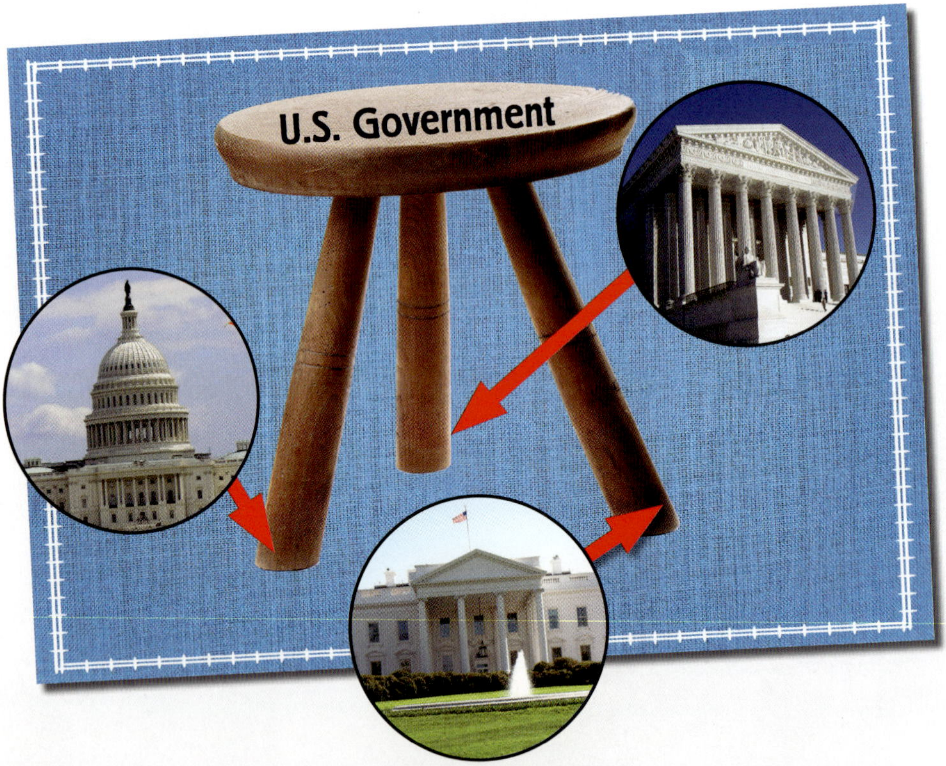

Three Branches

In this book, you learned about the three branches of government: the executive branch, the legislative branch, and the judicial branch. Tell a friend one thing you learned about each branch of our government.